How to Study the Bible

R. A. TORREY

PUBLISHER'S NOTE

Noted as one of the world's most outstanding Bible teachers, Dr. R.A. Torrey shares his wealth of knowledge in this easy-to-understand classic. It is our hope that this edited version will enrich your time alone with God.

HOW TO STUDY THE BIBLE

R.A. Torrey

Copyright © 1985 by Whitaker House
Printed in the United States of America
ISBN 0-88368-164-1

Edited by Donna C. Arthur

CONTENTS

INTRODUCTION

The Bible contains golden nuggets of truth, and anyone willing to dig for that truth is certain to find it.

Those reading this book for the first time must not become frightened at the elaborate methods I will suggest. They are not difficult. Their fruitfulness has been tested with those who have varying degrees of education, and the results have been found to be practical. As you use the methods I will recommend, you will soon find your ability to study the Bible rapidly increasing, until you will do more in fifteen minutes than you once could in an hour.

Although the Bible is read much, it is comparatively studied little. The methods you will learn are the same methods being used in highly technical fields such as science and medicine. First, you will make a careful analysis of the facts. Then, you will learn how to classify those facts. While we cannot all be students of technology, we can all be profound students of Scripture. No other book offers the opportunity for intellectual development by its study than the Bible. People who have studied little else other than the Scriptures have astonished and dismayed scholars and theologians.

The truths you will find as you study Scripture will far transcend any other study in inspiration, helpfulness, and practical value. They will, in fact, become life-changing!

Chapter 1

CONDITIONS FOR PROFITABLE BIBLE STUDY

While you will be learning profitable methods for Bible study, there is something more important, however, than the best procedures. The secret lies in meeting certain fundamental conditions before you begin to study God's Word. If you meet these conditions, you will get more out of the Bible, even while pursuing the poorest methods, than the one who does not meet them while he pursues the best methods. What you will need is far deeper than a new and better technique.

Obtaining Spiritual Understanding

The most essential of these conditions is that *you must be born again.* The Bible is a spiritual book. It combines spiritual things with spiritual words. Only a spiritual man can understand its deepest and most precious teachings. "The natural man receiveth not the things of the Spirit of God: for they are foolishness unto him: and he cannot know them, because they are spiritually discerned'' (1 Corinthians 2:14).

Spiritual discernment can be obtained in only one way, by being born again—''Except a man be born again, he cannot see the kingdom of God'' (John 3:3). No mere knowledge of the human languages in which the Bible was written, however extensive and accurate it may be, will qualify one to understand and appreciate the Bible. One must understand the divine language in which it was written as well as the language of the Holy Spirit.

A person who understands the language of the Holy Spirit, but who does not understand a word of Greek or Hebrew or Aramaic, will get more out of the Bible than one who knows all about Greek and Hebrew but is not born again. It is a well-demonstrated fact that many plain men and women who possess no knowledge of the original languages in which the Bible was written have a knowledge of the real contents of the Bible. Their understanding of its actual teaching and its depth, fullness, and beauty far surpasses that of many learned professors in theological faculties.

One of the greatest follies today is to allow an unregenerate person to teach the Bible. It would be just as unreasonable to allow someone to teach art because he had an accurate, technical knowledge of paints. An aesthetic sense is required to make a person a competent teacher of art. It requires spiritual sense to make a person a competent teacher of the Bible.

One who had aesthetic discernment but little or no

8

technical knowledge of paint would be a far more competent critic of works of art than one who had a great technical knowledge of paint but no aesthetic discernment. The person who has no technical knowledge of Greek and Hebrew but has spiritual discernment is a far more competent critic of the Bible than the one who has a rare, technical knowledge of Greek and Hebrew but no spiritual discernment.

It is unfortunate that more emphasis is often placed on a knowledge of Greek and Hebrew in training for the ministry than is placed on the spiritual life and its consequent spiritual discernment. Unregenerate men should not be forbidden to study the Bible, because the Word of God is the instrument the Holy Spirit uses in the new birth. (See 1 Peter 1:23 and James 1:18.) But it should be distinctly understood that, while there are teachings in the Bible the natural man can understand, its most distinctive and characteristic teachings are beyond his grasp. Its highest beauties belong to a world in which he has no vision.

The first fundamental condition for profitable Bible study then is "Ye must be born again" (John 3:7). You cannot study the Bible to the greatest profit if you have not been born again. Its best treasures are sealed to you.

Gaining A Spiritual Appetite

The second condition for profitable study is to have *a love for the Bible*. A man who eats with an

9

appetite will get far more good out of his meal than a man who eats from a sense of duty. A student of the Bible should be able to say with Job, "I have esteemed the words of his mouth more than my necessary food" (Job 23:12) or with Jeremiah, "Thy words were found and I did eat them; and thy word was unto me the joy and rejoicing of mine heart: for I am called by thy name, O Lord God of hosts" (Jeremiah 15:16).

Many come to the table God has spread in His Word with no appetite for spiritual food and go mincing here and there and grumbling about everything. Spiritual indigestion lies at the bottom of much modern criticism of the Bible.

But how can one get a love for the Bible? First of all by being born again. Where there is life, there is likely to be appetite. A dead man never hungers. This brings us back to the first condition. But going beyond this the more there is of vitality, the more there is of hunger. Abounding life means abounding hunger for the Word.

Study of the Word stimulates love for the Word. I remember when I had more appetite for books about the Bible than I had for the Bible itself; but with increasing study, there has come increasing love for the Book. Bearing in mind who the Author of the Book is, what its purpose is, what its power is, and what the riches of its contents are will go far toward stimulating a love and appetite for the Book.

Digging For Treasures

The third condition is a *willingness to work hard.* Solomon has given a graphic picture of the Bible student who gets the most profit out of his study. "My son, if thou wilt receive my words, and hide my commandments with thee; so that thou incline thine ear unto wisdom, and apply thine heart to understanding; yea, if thou criest after knowledge, and liftest up thy voice for understanding; if thou seekest . . . and searchest for her as for hid treasures; then shalt thou understand the fear of the Lord, and find the knowledge of God" (Proverbs 2:1-5).

Seeking for silver and searching for hidden treasure means hard work, and the one who wishes to get not only the silver but the gold as well out of the Bible must make up his mind to dig. It is not glancing at the Word but studying the Word, meditating upon the Word, and pondering the Word that brings the richest yields.

The reason many people get so little out of their Bible reading is simply because they are not willing to think. Intellectual laziness lies at the bottom of a large percent of fruitless Bible reading. People are constantly crying for new methods of Bible study, but what many of them want is simply some method of Bible study where they can get the most without much work.

If someone could tell lazy Christians some method of Bible study whereby they could put the sleepiest ten minutes of the day, just before they go to bed, into Bible study and get the most profit that God intends, that would be what they desire. But it can't be done. Men must be willing to work and work hard if they wish to dig out the treasures of infinite wisdom, knowledge, and blessing that He has stored up in His Word.

A business friend once asked me in a hurried call to tell him "in a word" how to study his Bible. I replied, "Think." The psalmist pronounces that man is "blessed" who "meditates in the law of the Lord, day and night." (See Psalm 1:2.) The Lord commanded Joshua to "meditate therein day and night" and assured him that as a result of this meditation "then thou shalt make thy way prosperous, and then thou shalt have good success" (Joshua 1:8). In this way alone can one study the Bible to the greatest profit.

One pound of beef well chewed, digested, and assimilated will give more strength than tons of beef merely glanced at; and one verse of Scripture chewed, digested, and assimilated will give more strength than whole chapters simply skimmed. Weigh every word you read in the Bible. Look at it. Turn it over and over. The most familiar passages take on new meaning in this way. Spend fifteen minutes on each word in Psalm 23:1 or Philippians 4:19 and see if it is not so.

Finding The Treasure's Keys

The fourth condition is *a will wholly surrendered to God*. Jesus said, "If any man will do his will, he shall know of the doctrine'' (John 7:17). A surrendered will gives that clearness of spiritual vision necessary to understand God's Book. Many of the difficulties and obscurities of the Bible rise simply because the will of the student is not surrendered to the will of the Author of the Book.

It is remarkable how clear, simple, and beautiful passages that once puzzled us become when we are brought to that place where we say to God, ''I surrender my will unconditionally to Yours. I have no will but Yours. Teach me Your will.'' A surrendered will does more to make the Bible an open book than a university education. It is simply impossible to get the largest profit out of your Bible study until you do surrender your will to God. You must be very definite about this.

Many will say, ''Oh, yes, my will is surrendered to God,'' but it is not. They have never gone alone with God and said intelligently and definitely to Him, ''O God, I here and now give myself up to You, for You to command me, lead me, shape me, send me, and do with me absolutely as You will.'' Such an act is a wonderful key to unlock the treasure house of God's Word. The Bible becomes a new Book when a man surrenders to God. Doing that brought a complete transformation in my own theology, life, and ministry.

Use It Or Lose It

The fifth condition is very closely related to the

fourth. The student of the Bible who would get the greatest profit out of his studies must be *obedient to its teachings as soon as he sees them*. It was good advice James gave to early Christians and to us, "Be ye doers of the word, and not hearers only, deceiving your own selves" (James 1:22).

Many who consider themselves Bible students are deceiving themselves in this way today. They see what the Bible teaches, but they do not do it; and they soon lose their power to see it. Truth obeyed leads to more truth. Truth disobeyed destroys the capacity for discovering truth.

There must be not only a general surrender of the will but specific, practical obedience to each new word of God discovered. No place is the law more joyously certain on the one hand and more sternly inexorable on the other than in the matter of using or refusing the truth revealed in the Bible. "Unto every one that hath shall be given, and he shall have abundance: but from him that hath not shall be taken away even that which he hath" (Matthew 25:29). Use, and you get more; refuse, and you lose all.

Do not study the Bible for the mere gratification of intellectual curiosity but to find out how to live and how to please God. Whatever duty you find commanded in the Bible, do it at once. Whatever good you see in any Bible character, imitate it immediately. Whatever mistake you note in the actions of Bible men and women, scrutinize your own life to see if you are making the same mistake; and if you find you are, correct it immediately.

James compares the Bible to a mirror. (See James 1:23-24.) The chief purpose of a mirror is to show you if anything is out of place about you. If you find there is, you can set it right. Use the Bible in that way.

Obeying the truth you already see will solve the enigmas in the verses you do not as yet understand. Disobeying the truth you see darkens the whole world of truth. This is the secret of much of the skepticism and error of the day. Men saw the truth, but did not do it; and now it is gone.

I once knew a bright and promising young minister who made rapid advancement in the truth. One day, however, he said to his wife, "It's nice to believe this truth, but we need not speak so much about it." He began to hide his testimony. Not long after this his wife died, and he began to drift. The Bible became to him a sealed book. His faith reeled, and he publicly renounced his belief in the fundamental truths of the Bible. He seemed to lose his grip even on the doctrine of immortality. What was the cause of it all? *Truth flees when it is not lived and stood for.* That man was admired by many and applauded by some, but light had given place to darkness in his soul.

Come As A Child

The sixth condition is *a childlike mind.* God reveals His deepest truths to babes. No age needs more than our own to lay to heart the words of

15

Jesus, "I thank thee, O Father, Lord of heaven and earth, because thou hast hid these things from the wise and prudent, and hast revealed them unto babes" (Matthew 11:25).

How can we be babes if God is to reveal His truth unto us, and we are to understand His Word? A child is not full of his own wisdom. He recognizes his ignorance and is ready to be taught. He does not oppose his own notions and ideas to those of his teachers.

It is in that spirit we should come to the Bible if we are to get the most profit out of our study. Do not come to the Bible seeking confirmation for your own ideas. Come rather to find out what God's ideas are as He has revealed them. Come not to find a confirmation of your own opinion but to be taught what God may be pleased to teach. If a man comes to the Bible just to find his notions taught there, he will find them. But if he comes, recognizing his own ignorance, just as a little child seeks to be taught, he will find something infinitely better than his own notions, even the mind of God.

We see why it is that many persons cannot see things that are plainly taught in the Bible. They are so full of their own ideas that there is no room left for what the Bible actually teaches.

An illustration of this is given in the lives of the apostles at one stage in their training. In Mark 9:31, we read, "For he taught his disciples and said unto them, The Son of man is delivered into the hands of men, and they shall kill him; and after that he is

16

killed, he shall rise the third day." Now that is as plain and definite as language can make it, but it was utterly contrary to the apostles' notions as to what would happen to Christ.

We read in the next verse, "They understood not that saying." Is this any different than our own inability to comprehend plain statements in the Bible when they run counter to our preconceived notions?

You must come to Christ like a child to be taught what to believe and do, rather than coming as a full-grown person who already knows it all and must find some interpretations of Christ's words that will fit into your mature and infallible philosophy. Many people are so full of unbiblical theology that it takes a lifetime to get rid of it and understand the clear teaching of the Bible. "Oh, what can this verse mean?" many bewildered cry. It means what it plainly says. But that person is not after the meaning God has manifestly put into it, but the meaning he can, by some ingenious trick of exegesis, twist to make it fit into his scheme.

Don't come to the Bible to find out what you can make it mean but to find out what God intended it to mean. People often miss the real truth of a verse by saying, "But that can be interpreted this way." Oh, yes, so it can, but is that the way God intended it to be interpreted?

We all need to pray, "Oh, God, make me a little child. Empty me of my own notions. Teach me Your own mind. Make me ready like a little child to receive all that You have to say, no matter how contrary it is to what I have thought before." How the Bible opens up to one who approaches it in that way! How it closes up to the fool who thinks he knows everything and imagines he can give points to Peter, Paul, and even to God Himself!

I was once talking with a ministerial friend about what seemed to be the clear teaching of a certain passage. "Yes," he replied, "but that doesn't agree with my philosophy." This man was sincere, yet he did not have the childlike spirit essential for productive Bible study. It is a great point gained in Bible study when we are brought to realize that an infinite God knows more than we, that our highest wisdom is less than the knowledge of the most ignorant babe compared with His, and that we must come to Him to be taught as babes.

We are not to argue with Him. But we so easily and so constantly forget this that every time we open our Bibles, we would do well to bow humbly before God and say, "Father, I am but a child, teach me."

Believing God's Word

The seventh condition of studying the Bible for the greatest profit is that we study it as *the Word of God*. The apostle Paul, in writing to the Thessalonians, thanked God without ceasing that when they received the Word of God, they "received it not as the word of men, but as it is in truth, the word of God" (1 Thessalonians 2:13). Paul thanked God for that, and so may we thank God when we get to the place where we receive the Word of God as *the* Word of God.

He who does not believe the Bible is the Word of God should be encouraged to study it. Once I doubted that the Bible was the Word of God, but the firm confidence that I have today that the Bible is the Word of God has come more from the study of the Book itself than from anything else. Those who doubt it are more usually those who study *about* the Book rather than those who dig into the actual teachings of the Book.

Studying the Bible as the Word of God involves four things.

1. It involves the *unquestioning acceptance of its teachings* when definitely ascertained, even when they may appear unreasonable or impossible. Reason demands that we submit our judgment and reasonings to the statements of infinite wisdom. Nothing is more irrational than rationalism which makes the finite wisdom the test of infinite wisdom and submits the teachings of God's omniscience to the approval of man's judgment. Conceit says, "This cannot be true, even though God says it, for it does not approve itself to *my* reason." "Nay but, O man, who art thou that repliest against God?" (Romans 9:20).

Real human wisdom, when it finds infinite wisdom, bows before it and says, "Speak what You will and I will believe." When we have once become convinced that the Bible is God's Word, its teach-

19

ings must be the end of all controversy and discussion. A "thus saith the Lord" will settle every question. Yet many who profess to believe that the Bible is the Word of God will shake their heads and say, "Yes, but I *think* so and so," or "Doctor____ or Professor____ or our church doesn't teach that way." There is little advantage to that sort of study.

2. Studying the Bible as the Word of God involves *absolute reliance upon all its promises* in all their length and breadth. The person who studies the Bible as the Word of God will not discount any one of its promises one iota. The one who studies the Bible as the Word of God will say, "God who cannot lie has promised," and he will not try to make God a liar by trying to make one of His promises mean less than it says. The one who studies the Bible as the Word of God will be on the lookout for promises. As soon as he finds one, he should seek to ascertain what it means and then place his entire trust upon its full meaning.

This is one of the secrets of profitable Bible study. Hunt for promises and appropriate them as fast as you find them by meeting the conditions and risking all upon them. This is the way to make all the fullness of God's blessing your own. This is the key to all the treasures of God's grace. Happy is the man who has so learned to study the Bible as God's Word that he is ready to claim for himself every new promise as it appears and to risk everything upon it.

3. Studying the Bible as the Word of God involves *prompt obedience to its every precept*. Obedience

may seem hard and impossible; but God has commanded it, and you have nothing to do but to obey and leave the results with God. To get results from your Bible study, resolve that, from this time on, you will claim every clear promise and obey every plain command. When the meaning of promises and commands are not yet clear, try to get their meaning made clear immediately.

4. Studying the Bible as the Word of God involves *studying it as in God's presence.* When you read a verse of Scripture, hear the voice of the living God speaking directly to you in these written words. There is new power and attractiveness in the Bible when you have learned to hear a living, present Person—God, our Father—talking directly to you in these words.

One of the most fascinating and inspiring statements in the Bible is "Enoch walked with God" (Genesis 5:24). We can have God's glorious companionship any moment we please by simply opening His Word and letting the living and ever-present God speak to us through it. With what holy awe and strange and unutterable joy one studies the Bible if he studies it in this way! It is heaven come down to earth.

The Key To Understanding

The last condition for profitable Bible study is *prayerfulness.* The psalmist prayed, "Open thou mine eyes, that I may behold wondrous things out

21

of thy law" (Psalm 119:18). Everyone who desires productive study needs to offer a similar prayer every time he undertakes the study of the Word. Few keys open many treasure chests of prayer. Few clues unravel many difficulties. Few microscopes disclose many beauties hidden from the eye of the ordinary observer. What new light often shines from an old familiar text as you bend over it in prayer!

I believe in studying the Bible many times on your knees. When you read an entire book through upon your knees—and this is easily done—that book takes on a new meaning and becomes a new book. You should never open the Bible without at least lifting your heart to God in silent prayer that He will interpret it and illumine its pages by the light of His Spirit. It is a rare privilege to study any book under the immediate guidance and instruction of the author, and this is the privilege of us all in studying the Bible.

When you come to a passage that is difficult to understand or difficult to interpret, instead of giving up or rushing to some learned friend or some commentary, lay that passage before God and ask Him to explain it. Plead God's promise, "If any of you lack wisdom, let him ask of God, that giveth to all men liberally, and upbraideth not; and it shall be given him. But let him ask in faith, nothing wavering" (James 1:5-6).

Harry Morehouse, one of the most remarkable Bible scholars among unlearned men, used to say that whenever he came to a passage in the Bible that he could not understand, he would search through the Bible for another passage that threw light upon it and lay it before God in prayer. He said he had never found a passage that did not yield to this treatment.

Some years ago I took a tour of Switzerland with a friend, visiting some of the more famous zoolithic caves. One day the country letter-carrier stopped us and asked if we would like to see a cave of rare beauty and interest, away from the beaten tracks of travel. Of course, we said, "Yes." He led us through the woods and underbrush to the mouth of the cave. As we entered, all was dark and uncanny. He expounded greatly on the beauty of the cave, telling us of altars and fantastic formations; but we could see absolutely nothing. Now and then he uttered a note to warn us to be careful as near our feet lay a gulf whose bottom had never been discovered. We began to fear that we might be the first discoverers of the bottom.

There was nothing pleasant about the whole affair. But as soon as a magnesium taper was lighted, all became different. Stalagmites rose from the floor to meet the stalactites descending from the ceiling. The great altar of nature that peasant fancy ascribed to the skill of ancient worshippers and the beautiful and fantastic formations on every hand all glistened in fairy-like beauty in the brilliant light.

I have often thought it was like a passage of Scripture. Others tell you of its beauty, but you cannot see it. It looks dark, intricate, forbidding, and dangerous; but when God's own light is kindled there by prayer, how different it all becomes in an instant. You see a beauty that language cannot express. Only those who have stood there in the same light can appreciate it. He who would understand and love his Bible must be much in prayer. Prayer will do more than a college education to make the Bible an open and glorious book.

Chapter 2

INDIVIDUAL BOOK STUDY

The first method of Bible study that we will consider is the *study of individual books*. This method of study is the most thorough and the most difficult, but the one that yields the most permanent results. We take it up first because, in the author's opinion, it should occupy the greater portion of our time.

How To Begin

The first step is selecting the correct book of the Bible to study. If you make an unfortunate selection, you may become discouraged and give up a method of study that might have been most fruitful.

A few points will be helpful to the beginner:

For your first book study, choose a short book. Choosing a long book to begin with leads to discouragement. The ordinary student will give it up before the final results are reached.

Choose a comparatively easy book. Some books of the Bible are harder to understand than others. You may want to meet and overcome these later, but it is not recommended work for a beginner. When you are more familiar with Scripture as a whole, then you can do this successfully and satisfactorily. You will soon find yourself floundering if you begin too soon.

The first epistle of Peter is an exceedingly precious book, but a few of the most difficult passages in the Bible are in it. If it were not for these difficult passages, it would be a good book to recommend to the beginner. In view of these difficulties, it is not wise to undertake it until later.

Choose a book that is rich enough in its teaching to illustrate the advantage of this method of study and thus give a keen appetite for further studies of the same kind. Once you have gone through one reasonably large book by the method of study about to be described, you will have an eagerness that will encourage you to find time for further studies.

A book that meets all the conditions stated is the first epistle of Paul to the Thessalonians. It is quite short, has no great difficulties in interpretation, and is exceedingly rich in its teaching. It has the further advantage of being the first of the Pauline Epistles. The first epistle of John is also a good book to begin with and is not difficult.

1 Thess
1 John

26

The second step is to master the general contents of the book. The method is very simple. It consists in merely reading the book through without stopping; then reading it through again and again, say a dozen times in all, at a single sitting. To one who has never tried this, it does not seem as if that would amount to much. But any thoughtful man who has ever tried it will tell you quite differently.

It is simply wonderful how a book takes on new meaning and beauty. It begins to open up. New relationships between different parts of the book begin to disclose themselves. Fascinating lines of thought running through the book appear. The book is grasped as a whole, and a foundation is laid for an intelligent study of those parts in detail.

Rev. James M. Gray of Boston, a prominent teacher and a great lover of the Bible, says that for many years of his ministry he had "an inadequate and unsatisfactory knowledge of the English Bible." The first practical idea he received in the study of the English Bible was from a layman. The brother possessed an unusual serenity and joy in his Christian experience, which he attributed to his reading of the letter to the Ephesians.

Mr. Gray asked him how he read it. He said he had taken a pocket copy of the Scripture into the woods one Sunday afternoon and read Ephesians through at a single sitting, repeating the process a dozen times before stopping. When he arose he had gotten possession of the epistle or, rather, its wondrous truths had gotten possession of him. This was the secret, simple as it was, that Mr. Gray had been waiting and praying for. From this time on Mr. Gray studied his Bible in this way, and it became a new book to him.

Practical Principles For Study

The third step is to prepare an introduction to the book. Write down at the top of separate sheets of paper or cards the following questions: (1) Who wrote this book? (2) To whom did he write it? (3) Where did he write it? (4) When did he write it? (5) What was the occasion of his writing? (6) What was the purpose for which he wrote? (7) What were the circumstances of the author when he wrote? (8) What were the circumstances of those to whom he wrote? (9) What glimpses does the book give into the life and character of the author? (10) What are the leading ideas of the book? (11) What is the central truth of the book? (12) What are the characteristics of the book?

Having prepared your sheets of paper with these headings, lay them side by side on your study table. Go through the book slowly, and, as you come to an answer to any one of these questions, write it down on the appropriate sheet of paper. It may be necessary to go through the book several times to do the work thoroughly and satisfactorily, but you will be amply rewarded. When you have finished your own work in this line, and not until then, it would be good to refer to commentaries to compare your results with those reached by others.

The introduction you prepare for yourself will be worth many times more to you than anything you can gain from the research of others. Your study will be a rare education of the facilities of perception, comparison, and reasoning.

Seeing The Big Picture

Sometimes the answers to our questions will be found in a related book. For example, if you are studying one of the Pauline Epistles, the answer to your questions may be found in the Acts of the Apostles or in another letter. Of course, all the questions given will not apply to every book in the Bible.

If you are not willing to give the time and effort necessary, this introductory work can be omitted but only at a great sacrifice. Single passages in an epistle can never be correctly understood unless we know to whom they were written. Much false interpretation of the Bible arises from taking a local application and applying it as universal authority. So, also, false interpretation often arises from applying to the unbeliever what was intended for the believer.

Note the occasion of the writing. It will clear up the meaning of a passage that would be otherwise obscure. Bearing in mind the circumstances of the author as he wrote will frequently give new force to his words.

The jubilant epistle to the Philippians contains repeated phrases such as: "rejoice in the Lord," "trust in the Lord," and "be anxious for nothing." Remember that these words were written by a prisoner awaiting possible sentence of death, and then they will become more meaningful to you.

If you will remember the main purpose for which a book was written, it will help you to interpret its incidental exhortations in their proper relationship. In fact, the answers to all the questions will be valuable in all the work that follows, as well as valuable in themselves.

Divide And Conquer

The fourth step is to divide the book into its proper sections. This procedure is not indispensable, but still it is valuable. Go through the book and notice the principal divisions in the thought. Mark them. Then go through these divisions and find if there are any natural subdivisions and mark them. In dividing your studies, work from a version of the Bible that is not chopped up by a purely mechanical and irrational verse division but divided according to a logical plan.

Having discovered the division of the book, proceed to give each section an appropriate caption. Make this caption as precise a statement of the general contents of the section as possible. Make it also as brief and as impressionable as possible so that it will fix itself in your mind. Create the captions of the subdivisions to connect with the general caption of the division. Do not attempt too elaborate a division at first.

The following division of First Peter, without many marked subdivisions, will serve as a simple illustration:

1. Chapter 1:1-2. Introduction and salutation to the pilgrims and sojourners in Pontus, etc.

2. Chapter 1:3-12. The inheritance reserved in heaven and the salvation ready to be revealed for those pilgrims who, in the midst of manifold temptations, are kept by the power of God through faith.

3. Chapter 1:13-25. The pilgrim's conduct during the days of his pilgrimage.

4. Chapter 2:1-10. The high calling, position, and destiny of the pilgrim people.

5. Chapter 2:11-12. The pilgrim's conduct during the days of his pilgrimage.

6. Chapter 2:13-17. The pilgrim's duty toward the human governments under which he lives.

7. Chapter 2:18-3:7. The duty of various classes of pilgrims.
   a. Chapter 2:18-25. The duty of servants toward their masters—enforced by an appeal to Christ's conduct under injustice and reviling.

b. Chapter 3:1-6. The duty of wives toward husbands.

c. Chapter 3:7. The duty of husbands toward their wives.

8. Chapter 3:8-12. The conduct of pilgrims toward one another.

9. Chapter 3:13-22. The pilgrim suffering for righteousness' sake.

10. Chapter 4:1-6. The pilgrim's separation from the practices of those among whom he spends the days of his pilgrimage.

11. Chapter 4:7-11. The pilgrim's sojourning drawing to a close and his conduct during the last days.

12. Chapter 4:12-19. The pilgrim suffering for and with Christ.

13. Chapter 5:1-4. The duty and reward of elders.

14. Chapter 5:5-11. The pilgrim's walk—humble, trustful, watchful, and steadfast—and a doxology.

15. Chapter 5:12-14. Conclusion and benediction.

Taking Bite-Size Pieces

The fifth step is to take each verse in order and study it. The first thing you must do in this verse-by-verse study of the book is to get the exact meaning of the verse. How is this to be done? Three steps lead into the meaning of a verse.

First, try to get the exact meaning of the words

used. You will find two classes of words: those whose meaning is perfectly apparent and those whose meaning is doubtful. It is quite possible to find the precise meaning of these doubtful words. This is not done, however, by consulting a dictionary. That is an easy, but dangerous, method of finding the scriptural significance of a word. The only safe and sure method is to study the usage of the word in the Bible itself and particularly in the Bible writer that you are studying.

To study the Bible usage of words, you must have a concordance. In my opinion, the best concordance is *Strong's Exhaustive Concordance of the Bible*. The next best is *Young's Analytical Concordance*. *Cruden's Complete Concordance* will do also if you are on a limited budget. When you are studying a particular word, all the passages in which the word occurs should be found and examined. In this way the precise meaning of the word will be determined.

Many important Bible doctrines will change the meaning of a word. For example, two schools of theology are divided on the meaning of the word "justify." The critical question is, does the word "justify" mean "to make righteous," or does it mean "to count or declare righteous"? The correct interpretation of many passages of Scripture hinges upon the sense which we give to this word. Look up all the passages in the Bible in which the word is found, and then you will have no doubt as to the Bible usage and meaning of the word. Deuteronomy 25:1, Exodus 23:7, Isaiah 5:23, Luke 16:15, Romans

2:13, 3:23-24, Luke 18:14, and Romans 4:2-8 will serve to illustrate the Biblical usage.

By using *Strong's* or *Young's Concordance,* you will see that the same word may be used in the English version as the translation of several Greek or Hebrew words. Of course, in determining the Biblical usage, we should give special attention to those passages in which the English word examined is the translation of the same word in Greek or Hebrew. Either of these concordances will enable you to do this, even though you are not acquainted with Greek or Hebrew. It will be much easier to do, however, with *Strong's Concordance* than *Young's.*

It is surprising how many knotty problems in the interpretation of Scripture are solved by the simple examination of the Biblical usage of words. For example, one of the burning questions of today is the meaning of 1 John 1:7. Does this verse teach that "the blood of Jesus Christ" cleanses us from all the guilt of sin; or does it teach us that "the blood of Jesus Christ" cleanses us from the very presence of sin so that, by the blood of Christ, indwelling sin is itself eradicated?

Many of those who read this question will answer it offhand at once, one way or the other. But the offhand way of answering questions of this kind is a bad way. Take your concordance and look up every passage in the Bible in which the word "cleanse" is used in connection with blood, and the question will be answered conclusively and forever.

Never conclude that you have the right meaning

34

of a verse until you have carefully determined the meaning of all doubtful words in it by an examination of Bible usage. Even when you are fairly sure you know the meaning of the words, it is good not to be too sure until you have looked it up.

Look Behind And Ahead

Now try to ascertain the meaning of a verse by carefully noticing the context (what goes before and what comes after). Many verses, if they stood alone, might be capable of several interpretations. But when the context is considered, all the interpretations except one are seen to be impossible.

For example, in John 14:18, Jesus said, "I will not leave you comfortless: I will come to you." What does Jesus mean when He says, "I will come to you"? One commentator says, "He refers to His reappearance to His disciples after His resurrection to comfort them." Another says, "He refers to His second coming." Another says, "He refers to His coming through the Holy Spirit's work to manifest Himself to His disciples and make His abode with them."

So what does Jesus mean? When doctors disagree can an ordinary layman decide? Yes, very often. Surely in this case. If you will carefully note what Jesus is talking about in the verses immediately preceding (verse 15-17) and immediately following (verses 19-26), you will have no doubt as to what coming Jesus refers to in this passage. You can see this by trying it for yourself.

Look At Comparison Verses

To ascertain the correct and precise meaning of a verse, examine parallel passages—passages that treat the same subject. For example, study other verses that give another account of the same event or passages that are evidently intended as a commentary on the passage in hand.

Very often, after having carefully studied the context, you may still be in doubt as to which interpretation the writer intended. In this case, there is a passage somewhere else in the Bible that will settle this question. In John 14:3, Jesus said, "I will come again, and receive you unto myself; that where I am, there ye may be also." A careful consideration of the words used in their relation to one another will help determine the meaning of this passage.

Still, among commentators, we find four different interpretations. First, the coming referred to here is explained as Christ's coming at death to receive the believer unto Himself, as in the case of Stephen. Another commentator interprets this as the coming again at the resurrection. A third sees the coming again through the Holy Spirit. And the last defines this passage to be when Christ returns personally and gloriously at the end of the age.

Which of these four interpretations is the correct one? What has already been said about verse 18 might seem to settle the question, but it does not. It is not at all clear that the coming in verse 3 is the same as in verse 18. What is said in connection with the two comings is altogether different. In the one case, it is a coming of Christ to "receive you unto myself; that where I am, there ye may be also." In the other case, it is a coming of Christ to manifest Himself unto us and make His abode with us.

Fortunately, there is a verse that settles the question. It is found in 1 Thessalonians 4:16-17. This will be clearly seen if we arrange the two passages in parallel columns.

John 14:3	1 Thessalonians 4:16-17
I will come again,	The Lord himself shall descend from heaven . . .
and receive you unto myself;	we . . . shall be caught up . . . to meet the Lord . . .
that where I am, there ye may be also.	so shall we ever be with the Lord.

The two passages manifestly match exactly in the three facts stated. Beyond a doubt, they refer to the same event. Look closely at 1 Thessalonians 4:16-17. There can be no doubt as to what coming of our Lord is referred to here.

These three steps lead us into the meaning of a verse. They require work, but it is work that anyone can do. When the meaning of a verse is thus settled, you can arrive at conclusions that are correct and fixed. After taking these steps, it is wise to consult commentaries to see how our conclusions agree with those of others.

Before we proceed to the next step after a verse's meaning has been determined, let me say that God intended to convey some definite truth in each verse of Scripture. With every verse of Scripture, we should ask what was this *intended* to teach, not what can this be *made* to teach; and we should not be satisfied until we have settled that. Of course, I admit a verse may have a primary meaning and then other more remote meanings. For example, a prophecy may have its primary fulfillment in some personage or event near at hand, such as Solomon, with a more remote and complete fulfillment in Christ.

Analyzing The Verse

We are not finished with a verse when we have determined its meaning. The next thing to do is to analyze the verse.

The way to do it is this: Look steadfastly at the verse and ask yourself, "What does this verse teach?" Then begin to write down: This verse teaches, 1st,____; 2nd,____; 3rd,____, etc. At first glance you will see one or two things the verse teaches; but as you look again and again, the teachings will begin to multiply. You will wonder how one verse could teach so much, and you will have an ever-growing sense of the divine Author of the Book.

I was once told the story of a professor who had a young man come to him to study ichthyology. The professor gave him a fish to study and told him to come back to get another lesson when he had mastered that fish. In time the young man came back and told the professor what he had observed about the fish. When he had finished, to his surprise, he was given the same fish again and told to study it further. He came back again, having observed new facts about the fish. But again he was given the same fish to study; and so it went on, lesson after lesson, until that student had been taught what his perceptive faculties were for and also how to do thorough work.

We ought to study the Bible in the same way. We ought to come back to the same verse of the Bible again and again until we have gotten, as far as it is possible to us, all that is in the verse. Then the probability is that when we come back to the same verse several months later, we will find something we did not see before.

An illustration of this method of analysis will be helpful. Look at 1 Peter 1:1-2. (Here is an instance in which the verse division of the King James Version is so manifestly illogical and absurd that in our analysis we cannot follow it but must take the two

verses together. This will often be the case.)
These verses teach:

1. This epistle was written by Peter.
2. The Peter who wrote this epistle was an apostle of Jesus Christ.(*Apostle* is Greek for the word missionary.)
3. Peter delighted to think and speak of himself as one sent of Jesus Christ. (Compare 2 Peter 1:1.)
4. The name—Jesus Christ—is used twice in these two verses. Its significance:
   a. Savior.
   b. Anointed One.
   c. Fulfiller of the messianic predictions of the Old Testament. It has special reference to the earthly reign of Christ.
5. This epistle was written to the elect, especially to the elect who are sojourners of the dispersion in Pontus, i.e., Paul's old field of labor.
6. Believers are:
   a. Elect or chosen of God.
   b. Foreknown of God.
   c. Sanctified of the Spirit.
   d. Sprinkled by the blood of Jesus Christ.
   e. Sojourners or pilgrims on earth.
   f. Subjects of multiplied grace.
   g. Possessors of multiplied peace.
7. Election. Who are the elect? Believers. (Compare verse 5.) To what are they elect? Obedience and the sprinkling of the blood of Jesus.

According to what are they elect? The foreknowledge of God. (Compare Romans 8:29-30.) In what are they elect? Sanctification of the Spirit. The test of election is obedience. (Compare 2 Peter 1:10.) The work of the three Persons of the Trinity in election are: The Father foreknows, Jesus Christ cleanses sin by His blood, and the Spirit sanctifies.

8. God is the Father of the elect.
9. The humanity of Christ is seen in the mention of His blood.
10. The reality of the body of Jesus Christ is seen in the mention of His blood.
11. It is by His blood and not by His example that Jesus Christ delivers from sin.
12. Peter's first and great wish and prayer for those to whom he wrote was that grace and peace might be multiplied.
13. It is not enough to have grace and peace. One should have multiplied grace and peace.
14. That one already has grace and peace is no reason to cease praying for them, but rather an incentive to prayer that they may have more grace and peace.
15. Grace precedes peace. Compare all passages where these words are found together.

This is simply an illustration of what is meant by analyzing a verse. The whole book should be gone through in this way.

Three rules must be observed, however, in this analytical work. First, do not put anything into your analysis that is not clearly in the verse. One of the greatest faults in Bible study is reading into passages what God never put into them. Some men have their pet doctrines; and they see them everywhere, even where God does not see them. No matter how true, precious, or scriptural a doctrine is, do not put into your analysis what is not in the verse. Considerable experience in this kind of study leads me to emphasize this rule.

Secondly, find all that is in the verse. This rule can only be carried out relatively. Much will escape you because many of the verses of the Bible are so deep. But do not rest until you have dug and dug and dug and there seems to be nothing more to find.

Then, state what you do find just as accurately and exactly as possible. Do not be content with putting into your analysis something *similar* to what is in the verse, but state in your analysis *precisely* what is in the verse.

Classifying Your Results

By your verse-by-verse analysis, you have discovered and recorded a great number of facts. The work now is to get these facts into an orderly shape. To do this, go carefully through your analysis and note the various subjects in the epistle. Write these subjects down as fast as noted. Having made a complete list of the subjects treated in the book, write these subjects on separate cards or sheets of paper. Then, go through the analysis again and copy each point in the analysis on its appropriate sheet of paper. For example, write every point regarding God the Father on the card.

This general classification should be followed by a more thorough and minute subdivision. Suppose that you are studying First Peter. Having completed your analysis of the epistle and gone over it carefully, you will find that the following subjects are treated in the epistle: (1) God; (2) Jesus Christ; (3) The Holy Spirit; (4) The Believer; (5) Wives and Husbands; (6) Servants; (7) The New Birth; (8) The Word of God; (9) Old Testament Scripture; (10) The Prophets; (11) Prayer; (12) Angels; (13) The Devil; (14) Baptism; (15) The Gospel; (16) Salvation; (17) The World; (18) Gospel Preachers and Teachers; (19) Heaven; (20) Humility; (21) Love.

These will serve for general headings. After the material found in the analysis is arranged under these headings, you will find it easier to divide it now into numerous subdivisions. For example, the material under the heading *God* can be divided into these subdivisions:

1. His names. The material under this heading is quite rich.
2. His attributes. This should be subdivided again: His holiness, His power, His foreknowledge, His faithfulness, His long-suffering, His grace, His mercy, His impartiality, and His severity.
3. God's judgments.

4. God's will.
5. What is acceptable to God?
6. What is due to God?
7. God's dwelling place.
8. God's dominion.
9. God's work or what God does.
10. The things of God. For example, "The mighty hand of God," "the house of God," "the gospel of God," "the flock of God," "the people of God," "the bondservants of God," "the Word of God," "the oracles of God," etc., etc.

To illustrate the classified arrangement of the teaching of a book on one doctrine will probably show you better how to do this work than any abstract statement. It will also illustrate in part how fruitful this method of study is. Look again at 1 Peter and its teachings regarding the believer.

I. THE BELIEVER'S PRIVILEGES

A. His election.
1. He is foreknown of the Father, 1:2.
2. He is elect or chosen of God, 1:2.
3. He is chosen of God according to His foreknowledge, 1:2.
4. He is chosen unto obedience, 1:2.
5. He is chosen unto the sprinkling of the blood of Jesus, 1:2.
6. He is chosen in sanctification by the Spirit, 1:2.

B. His calling.
   1. By whom called: God, 1:15; and the God of all grace, 5:10.
   2. To what called: The imitation of Christ in the patient taking of suffering for well doing, 2:20-21; To render blessing for reviling, 3:9; Out of darkness into God's marvelous light, 2:9; To God's eternal glory, 5:10.
   3. In whom called: In Christ, 5:10.
   4. The purpose of his calling: That he may show forth the praises of Him who called, 2:9; That he may inherit a blessing, 3:9.

C. His regeneration.
   1. Of God, 1:3.
   2. Unto a living hope, 1:3.
   3. Unto an inheritance incorruptible, undefiled, and that fadeth not away, reserved in heaven, 1:4.
   4. By the resurrection of Jesus Christ, 1:3.
   5. Of incorruptible seed by the Word of God that liveth, etc., 1:23.

D. His redemption.
   1. Not with corruptible things, as silver and gold, 1:18.
   2. With precious blood, even the blood of Christ, 1:19.
   3. From his vain manner of life, handed down from his father, 1:18.

4. His sins have been borne by Christ, in His own body, on the tree, 2:24.

E. His sanctification by the Spirit, 1:2.

F. His cleansing by the blood, 1:2.

G. His security.
   1. He is guarded by the power of God, 1:5.
   2. He is guarded unto a salvation ready, or prepared, to be revealed in the last time, 1:5.
   3. God careth for him, 5:7.
   4. He can cast all his anxiety upon God, 5:7.
   5. The God of all grace will perfect, establish, and strengthen him after a brief trial of suffering, 5:10.
   6. None can harm him if he is zealous of that which is good, 3:13.
   7. He shall not be put to shame, 2:6.

H. His joy.
   1. The character of his joy. Presently it is: an unspeakable joy, 1:8; and a joy full of glory, 1:8. This present joy cannot be hindered by being put to grief because of manifold temptations, 1:6. His future joy: exceeding, 4:13.
   2. He rejoices in: the salvation prepared

to be revealed in the last time, 1:5; his faith in the unseen Jesus Christ, 1:8; and in fellowship in Christ's sufferings, 4:13.

3. What he shall rejoice in: the revelation of Christ's glory, 4:13. Present joy in fellowship with the sufferings of Christ is the condition of exceeding joy at the revelation of Christ's glory, 4:13.

I. His hope.
1. Its character: A living hope, 1:3; a reasonable hope, 3:15; an inward hope, "in you," 3:15.
2. In whom is his hope: In God, 1:21.
3. The foundation of his hope: The resurrection of Jesus Christ, 1:3-21.

J. His salvation.
1. A past salvation: has been redeemed, 1:18-19; and has been healed, 2:24. By baptism, after a true likeness as Noah by the flood, the believer has passed out of the old life of nature into the new resurrection life of grace, 3:21.
2. A present salvation: He is *now* receiving the salvation of his soul, 1:9.
3. A *growing* salvation: through feeding on His Word, 2:2.
4. A *future* salvation: ready or prepared to be revealed in the last time, 1:5.

K. The believer's possessions.
1. God as his Father, 1:17.
2. Christ as his: Sin bearer, 2:24; Example, 2:21; Fellow sufferer, 4:13.
3. A living hope, 1:3.
4. An incorruptible, undefiled, and unfading inheritance reserved in heaven, 1:4.
5. Multiplied grace and peace, 1:2.
6. Spiritual milk without guile for his food, 2:2.
7. Gifts for service—each believer has, or may have, some gift, 4:10.

L. What believers are.
1. Sojourners or strangers, 1:1.
2. A sojourner on his way to another country, 2:1.
3. A holy priesthood, 2:5.
4. Living stones, 2:5.
5. A spiritual house, 2:5.
6. A chosen generation, 2:9.
7. A royal priesthood, 2:9.
8. A holy nation, 2:9.
9. Partakers of, or partners in, Christ's sufferings, 4:13.
10. A Christian: representative of Christ, 4:16.
11. The house of God, 4:17.
12. Partakers of, or partners in, the glory to be revealed, 5:1.
13. The flock of God, 5:2.

M. The believer's possibilities.
   1. He may die unto sin, 2:24.
   2. He may live unto righteousness, 2:24.
   3. He may follow in Christ's steps, 2:21.
   4. He may cease from sin, 4:1.
   5. He may cease from living to the lusts of men, 4:2.
   6. He may live unto the will of God, 4:2.

N. What was for the believer.
   1. The ministry of the prophets was in his behalf, 1:12.
   2. The preciousness of Jesus is for him, 2:7.

O. Unclassified.
   1. The gospel has been preached to him in the Holy Ghost, 1:12.
   2. Grace is to be brought unto him at the revelation of Jesus Christ, 1:3, compare Ephesians 3:7.
   3. He has tasted that the Lord is gracious, 2:3.

II. THE BELIEVER'S SUFFERINGS AND TRIALS.

A. The fact of the believer's sufferings and trials, 1:6.

B. The nature of the believer's sufferings and trials.
   1. He endures griefs, suffering wrongfully, 2:19.

2. He suffers for righteousness' sake, 3:14.
3. He suffers for well doing, 3:17; 2:20.
4. He suffers as a Christian, 4:16.
5. He is subjected to manifold temptations, 1:6.
6. He is put to grief in manifold temptations, 1:6.
7. He is spoken against as an evil doer, 2:12.
8. His good manner of life is reviled, 3:16.
9. He is spoken evil of because of his separated life, 4:4.
10. He is reproached for the name of Christ, 4:14.
11. He is subjected to fiery trials, 4:12.

C. Encouragements for believers undergoing fiery trials and suffering.
   1. It is better to suffer for well doing than for evil doing, 3:17.
   2. Judgment must begin at the house of God. The present judgment of believers through trial is not comparable to the future end of those who obey not the gospel, 4:17.
   3. Blessed is the believer who does suffer for righteousness' sake, 3:14, compare Matthew 5:10-12.
   4. Blessed is the believer who is

reproached for the name of Christ, 4:14.

5. The Spirit of Glory and the Spirit of God rests upon the believer who is reproached for the name of Christ, 4:14.

6. The believer's grief is for a little while, 1:6, R.V.

7. Suffering for a little while will be followed by God's glory in Christ, which is eternal, 5:10.

8. The suffering endured for a little while is for the testing of faith, 1:7.

9. The fiery trial is for a test, 4:12.

10. The faith thus proved is more precious than gold, 1:7.

11. Faith proven by manifold temptations will be found unto praise and honor and glory at the revelation of Jesus Christ, 1:7.

12. His proved faith may be found unto praise and glory and honor at the revelation of Jesus Christ, that the believer is for a little while subjected to manifold temptations, 1:7.

13. It is pleasing to God when a believer takes it patiently, when he does well and suffers for it, 2:20.

14. Through suffering in the flesh, we cease from sin, 4:1.

15. Those who speak evil of us shall

give account to God, 4:5.

16. Sufferings are being shared by fellow believers, 5:9.

17. Christ suffered for us, 2:21.

18. Christ suffered for sins once (or once for all), the righteous for the unrighteous, that He might bring us to God, being put to death in the flesh, but quickened in the spirit, 3:18.

19. Christ left the believer an example that he should follow in His steps, 2:21.

20. In our fiery trials we are made partakers of, or partners in, Christ's sufferings, 4:13.

21. When His glory is revealed, we shall be glad also with exceeding joy, 4:13.

D. How the believer should meet his trial and sufferings.

1. The believer should not regard his fiery trial as a strange thing, 4:12.

2. The believer should expect fiery trial, 4:12.

3. When the believer suffers as a Christian, let him not be ashamed, 4:16.

4. When the believer suffers as a Christian, let him glorify God in this name, 4:16.

5. When the believer suffers, let him not return reviling with reviling, or suffering with threatening, but commit him-

self to Him that judgeth righteously, 2:23.

6. When the believer suffers, he should commit the keeping of his soul unto God, as unto a faithful Creator, 4:19.

III. THE BELIEVER'S DANGERS.

A. The believer may fall into fleshly lusts that war against the soul, 2:11.

B. The believer may sin, 2:20.

C. The believer may fall into sins of the gravest character, 4:15. (Note in this verse the awful possibilities that lie dormant in the heart of a sincere, professed believer.)

D. The believer's prayers may be hindered, 3:7.

E. The believer is in danger that his high calling and destiny may tempt him to despise human laws and authority, 2:13.

F. The believer is in danger that his high calling may lead him to lose sight of his lowly obligations to human masters, 2:18.

G. Young believers are in danger of disregarding the will and authority of older believers, 5:5.

IV. THE BELIEVER'S RESPONSIBILITY.

A. Each believer has an individual responsibility, 4:10.

B. Each believer's responsibility is for the gift he has received, 4:10.

V. THE BELIEVER'S DUTIES.

A. What the believer should be.

1. Be holy in all manner of living because God is holy, 1:15; and because it is written, "Be ye holy," 1:16.
2. Be like Him who called him, 1:15-16.
3. Be sober (or of a calm, collected, thoughtful spirit), 1:13; 4:7; 5:8.
4. Be sober unto prayer, 4:7.
5. Be of a sound mind because the end of all things is approaching, 4:7.
6. Be watchful, 5:8.
7. Be steadfast in the faith, 5:9.
8. Be subject to every ordinance of man: for the Lord's sake, 2:13; to the king, as supreme, 2:13; to governors, as sent by the king for the punishment of evil-

doers, and for praise to them that do well, 2:14; because this is God's will, 2:15.

9. Be like-minded, 3:8.

10. Be sympathetic, 3:8.

11. Be tenderhearted, 3:8.

12. Be humble-minded, 3:8.

13. Be ready: always; to give an answer to every man that asketh a reason of the hope that is in him; with meekness and fear; in order to put to shame those who revile their good manner of life in Christ, 3:16.

14. Be not troubled, 3:14.

B. What the believer should not do.

1. The believer should not fashion himself according to the lusts of the old life of ignorance, 1:14.

2. The believer should not render evil for evil, 3:9.

3. The believer should not render reviling for reviling, 3:9.

4. The believer should not fear the world's fear, 3:14.

5. The believer should not live his remaining time in the flesh to the lusts of men, 4:2.

C. What the believer should do.
   1. Live as a child of obedience, 1:14.
   2. Pass the time of his sojourning here in fear, 1:17.
   3. Abstain from fleshly lusts that war against the soul, 2:11.
   4. Observe God's will as the absolute law of life, 2:15.
   5. Let his conscience be governed by the thought of God and not by the conduct of men, 2:19.
   6. Sanctify Christ in his heart as Lord, 3:15; compare Isaiah 8:13.
   7. Live his remaining time in the flesh to the will of God, 4:2.
   8. Put away: all malice, 2:1; all guile, 2:1; hypocrisies, 2:1; envies, 2:1; all evil speaking, 2:1.
   9. Come unto the Lord as unto a living stone, 2:4.
   10. Show forth the excellencies of Him who called him out of darkness into His marvelous light, 2:9.
   11. Arm himself with the mind of Christ: i.e. to suffer in the flesh, 4:1.
   12. Cast all his care upon God because He careth for him, 5:7.
   13. Stand fast in the true grace of God, 5:12.
   14. Withstand the devil, 5:9.
   15. Humble himself under the mighty

hand of God, 5:5: because God resisteth the proud and giveth grace unto the humble, 5:5-6; that God may exalt him in due time, 5:6.

16. Glorify God when he suffers as a Christian, 4:16.

17. See to it that he does not suffer as a thief or as an evildoer or as a meddler in other men's matters, 4:15.

18. Rejoice in fiery trial, 4:13.

19. Toward various persons: toward *God*—fear, 2:17; toward the *king*—honor, 2:17; toward *masters*—be in subjection with all fear (not only to the good and gentle, but to the froward) 2:18: toward the *brotherhood*—love, 1:22; 2:17; 4:8; toward his *revilers*—blessing for reviling, 3:9; toward the *Gentiles*—seemly behavior, 2:12 (that God may be glorified); toward *foolish men*—by well doing put to silence their ignorance, 2:15; and toward *all men*—honor, 2:17.

20. Long for the sincere milk of the Word, 2:2.

21. Gird up the loins of his mind, 1:13.

22. Grow, 2:2.

23. Hope perfectly on the grace to be brought unto him at the revelation of Jesus Christ, 1:13.

VI. THE BELIEVER'S CHARACTERISTICS.

A . His faith and hope is in God, 1:21.

B . Believes in God through Jesus Christ, 1:21.

C . Calls on God as Father, 1:17.

D . Believes in Christ, though he has never seen Him, 1:8.

E . Loves Christ though he has never seen Him, 1:8.

F . Is returned unto the Shepherd and Bishop of his soul, 2:25.

G . Has purified his soul in obedience to the truth, 1:22.

H . Has unfeigned love for the brethren, 1:22.

I . Has a good manner of life, 3:16.

J . Does not run with the Gentiles among whom he lives, to the same excess of riot and lives a separated life, 4:4.

K . Refrains his tongue from evil, 3:10. Refrains his lips that they speak no guile, 3:10.

L. Turns away from evil, 3:11.

M. Does good, 3:11.

N. Seeks peace, 3:11.

O. Pursues peace, 3:11.

VII. THE BELIEVER'S WARFARE.

A. The believer has a warfare before him, 4:1.

B. The mind of Christ is the proper armament for this warfare, 4:1.

C. The warfare is with the devil, 5:8-9.

D. Victory is possible for the believer, 5:9.

E. Victory is won through steadfastness in the faith, 5:9.

How To Retain Your Studies

At first thought it may seem that when we had completed our classification of results our work was finished, but this is not so. These results are for use: first, for personal enjoyment and appropriation, and afterward to give to others. To obtain results you must meditate upon them.

We are no more through with a book when we

have carefully and fully classified its contents than we are through with a meal when we have arranged it in an orderly way upon the table. It is there to eat, digest, and assimilate.

One of the greatest failures in Bible study today is at this point. There is observation, analysis, classification, but no meditation. Perhaps nothing is as important in Bible study as meditation. (See Joshua 1:8; Psalm 1:2-3.)

Take your classified teachings and go slowly over them. Ponder them, point by point, until these wonderful truths live before you and sink into your soul and become part of your life. Do this again and again. Nothing will go further than meditation to make you become a great, fresh, and original thinker and speaker. Very few people in this world are great thinkers.

The method of study outlined in this chapter can be shortened to suit the time and vocation of the student. For example, you can omit the verse-by-verse study and proceed at once to go through the book as a whole and note its teachings on different doctrines. This will greatly shorten and lighten the work. It will also greatly detract from the richness of the results, however, and will not be as thorough, accurate, or as scholarly. But any man can be, if he will, a scholar, at least in the most important things—that of Biblical study.

Chapter 3

TOPICAL STUDY

A second method of Bible study is the *topical method*. This consists in searching through the Bible to find out what its teaching is on various topics. It is perhaps the most fascinating of all the methods.

The only way to master any topic is to go through the Bible and find what it has to teach on that topic. Almost any great subject will take a remarkable hold upon the heart of a Christian, if you will take time to go through the Bible, from Genesis to Revelation, and note what it has to say on that topic. You will have a more full and more correct understanding of that topic than you ever had before.

D. L. Moody once said that he studied the word "grace" in this way. Day after day he went through the Bible studying what it had to say about "grace." As the Bible doctrine unfolded before his mind, his heart began to burn; until at last, full of the subject and on fire with the subject, he ran on to the street. Taking hold of the first man he met, he said, "Do you know grace?"

"Grace who?" was the reply.

"The grace of God that bringeth salvation." Then he poured out his soul on that subject.

If any child of God will study "grace" or "love" or "faith" or "prayer" or any other great Bible doctrine in this way, his soul, too, will become full of it. Jesus evidently studied the Old Testament scriptures in this way. "Beginning at Moses and all the prophets, he expounded unto them in all the scriptures the things concerning himself" (Luke 24:27). This method of study made the hearts of the two who walked with Him burn within them. (See Luke 24:32.) Paul seemed to have followed his Master in this method of study and teaching. (See Acts 17:2-3.)

Watch Out For Imbalance

This method of topical study has its dangers, however. Many are drawn by the fascination of this method to give up all other methods of study, and this is a great misfortune. A well-rounded, thorough knowledge of the Bible is not possible by this method of study. No one method of study is sufficient if you desire to be a well-rounded and well-balanced Bible student.

But the greatest danger lies in this: every man is almost certain to have some topics in which he is especially interested. If he studies his Bible topically, unless he is warned, he is more than likely to go over certain topics again and again. Thus, he will be very strong in this line of truth, but other topics of equal importance may be neglected, and he may become a one-sided man.

We never know one truth correctly until we know it in its proper relationship to other truths. I know of people, for example, who are interested in the great doctrine of the Lord's second coming. Therefore, almost all their Bible studies are on that line. Now this is a precious doctrine, but there are other doctrines in the Bible which a man needs to know; and it is folly to study this doctrine alone.

I know others whose whole interest and study seems to center in the subject of "divine healing." One man confided to a friend that he had devoted years to the study of the number "seven" in the Bible. This is doubtless an extreme case, but it illustrates the danger in topical study. It is certain that we will never master the whole range of Bible truth if we pursue the topical method alone. A few rules concerning topical study will probably be helpful to you.

Don't follow your fancy in the choice of topics. Don't take up any topic that happens to suggest itself. Make a list of all the subjects you can think of that are touched upon in the Bible. Make it as comprehensive and complete as possible. Then study these topics one by one in logical order. The following list of subjects is given as a suggestion. Each person can add to the list for himself and separate the general subjects into proper subdivisions.

LIST OF TOPICS

GOD

God as a Spirit
The unity of God
The eternity of God
The omnipresence of God
The personality of God
The omnipotence of God
The omniscience of God
The holiness of God
The love of God
The righteousness of God
The mercy or lovingkindness of God
The faithfulness of God
The grace of God

JESUS CHRIST

The divinity of Christ
The subordination of Christ to God
The human nature of Jesus Christ
The character of Jesus Christ
　　His holiness
　　His love to God
　　His love to man
　　His love for souls
　　His compassion
　　His prayerfulness
　　His meekness and humility

The death of Jesus Christ
    The purpose of Christ's death
    Why did Christ die?
    For whom did Christ die?
    The results of Christ's death

The resurrection of Jesus Christ
    The fact of the resurrection
    The results of the resurrection
    The importance of the resurrection
    The manner of the resurrection

The ascension and exaltation of Christ

The return or coming again of Christ
    The fact of His coming again
    The manner of His coming again
    The purpose of His coming again
    The result of His coming again
    The time of His coming again

The reign of Jesus Christ

THE HOLY SPIRIT

Personality of the Holy Spirit
Deity of the Holy Spirit
Distinction of the Holy Spirit
Subordination of the Holy Spirit
Names of the Holy Spirit
Work of the Holy Spirit
    In the universe

In man in general
In the believer
In the prophet and apostle
In Jesus Christ

MAN

His original condition
His fall
Man's standing before God
The future destiny of unbelievers
Justification
The new birth
Adoption
The believer's assurance of salvation
The flesh
Sanctification
Cleansing
Consecration
Faith
Repentance
Prayer
Thanksgiving
Praise
Worship
Love to God
Love to Jesus Christ
Love to man
The future destiny of believers

ANGELS

Their nature and position
Their number
Their abode
Their character
Their work
Their destiny

SATAN OR THE DEVIL

His existence
His nature and position
His abode
His work
Our duty regarding him
His destiny

DEMONS

Their existence
Their nature
Their work
Their destiny

For a student who has the perseverance to carry it through, it might be recommended to begin with the first topic on a list like this and go right through to the end, searching for everything the Bible has to say on these topics. I have done this and, thereby, gained a fuller knowledge of truth along these lines than I ever obtained by extended studies in systematic theology.

Many, however, will stagger at the *seeming* immensity of the undertaking. To such it is recommended to begin by selecting those topics that seem more important, but sooner or later settle down to a thorough study of what the Bible has to teach about God and man.

Be Thorough

Whenever you are studying any topic, do not be content with examining some of the passages in the Bible that bear upon the subject. As far as possible, find every passage in the Bible that bears on this subject. As long as there is a single passage in the Bible on any subject that you have not considered, you have not yet gotten a thoroughly true knowledge of that subject.

How can you find all the passages in the Bible that bear on any subject? First, by the use of a concordance. Look up every passage that has the word in it. Then look up every passage that has synonymous words in it. If, for example, you are studying the subject of prayer, look up every passage that has the word "pray" and its derivatives in it and also every passage that has such words as "cry," "call," "ask," "supplication," "intercession," etc., in it.

You may also use a Bible text book. A text book arranges the passages of Scripture, not by the words used, but by the subjects treated. Many verses on prayer do not have the word "prayer" or any synonymous word in them.

Lastly, passages not discovered by the use of either concordance or text book will come to light as you study by books or as you read the Bible through, and so our treatment of topics will be ever broadening.

Getting The Exact Meaning

Study each passage in its context and find its meaning in the way suggested in the chapter on "Individual Book Study."

Topical study is frequently carried on in a very careless fashion. Passages taken out of context are strung or huddled together because of some superficial connection with one another without regard to their real sense and teaching.

This has brought the whole method of topical study into disrepute. But it is possible to be as exact and scholarly in topical study as in any other method when the results are instructive and gratifying and not misleading. But the results are sure to be misleading and unsatisfactory if the work is done in a careless, inexact way.

How To Arrange Your Notes

In studying any large subject, you will obtain a large amount of written material. Having obtained it, it must now be organized into a logical study form. As you look it over carefully, you will soon see the facts that belong together. Arrange them together in a logical order.

For instance, perhaps you have accumulated much material on the Deity of Jesus Christ. An example of topical study may be arranged as follows:

JESUS CHRIST: HIS DEITY

I. Divine names

A. "The Son of God." (See Luke 22:70.) This name is given to Christ forty times. Besides this the synonymous expression, "His Son" or "My Son" are of frequent occurrence. This name of Christ is a distinctly divine name appearing in John 5:18.

B. "The only begotten Son." (See John 1:18.) This occurs five times. It is not true when people say that Jesus Christ is the Son of God only in the same sense that all men are sons of God. Compare Mark 12:6. Here Jesus Himself, having spoken of all the prophets as servants of God, speaks of Himself as "One," "a beloved Son."

C. "The first and the last." (See Revelation 1:17. Compare Isaiah 41:4; 44:6.) In these latter passages, it is "Jehovah," "Jehovah of hosts," who is "the first and the last."

D. "The Alpha and Omega" or "the beginning and the ending." (See Revelation 22:12,13,16.) In Revelation 1:8, it is the Lord who is the Alpha and Omega.

E. "The Holy One." (See Acts 3:14.) In Hosea 11:9 and many other passages, it is God who is "the Holy One."

F. "The Lord." (See Malachi 3:1; Luke 2:11; Acts 9:17; John 20:28; and Hebrews 1:10.) This name or title is used of Jesus several hundred times. He is spoken of as "*the* Lord" just as God is. Compare Acts 4:26 with 4:33. Note also Matthew 22:43-45, Philippians 2:11, and Ephesians 4:5. If anyone doubts the attitude of the apostles of Jesus toward Him as divine, they would do well to read one after another the passages which speak of Him as Lord.

G. "Lord of all." (See Acts 10:36.)

H. "The Lord of Glory." (See 1 Corinthians 2:8.) In Psalm 24:8-10, it is "the Lord of Hosts" who is the King of Glory.

I. "Wonderful," "Counseller," "Mighty God," "Everlasting Father," and "Prince of Peace." (See Isaiah 9:6.)

J. "God." (See Hebrews 1:8.) In John 20:27, Thomas calls Jesus "my God" and is gently rebuked for not believing it before.

K. "God with us." (See Matthew 1:23.)

L. "The great God." (See Titus 2:13.)

M. "God blessed forever." (See Romans 9:5.)

Conclusion: *Sixteen names clearly implying Deity are used of Christ in the Bible, some of them over and over again, the total number of passages reaching into the hundreds.*

II. Divine Attributes

A. Omnipotence.
1. Jesus has power over disease. It is subject to His word. (See Luke 4:39.)
2. The Son of God has power over death. It is subject to His word. (See Luke 7:14-15; 8:54-55; and John 5:25.)
3. Jesus has power over the winds and sea. They are subject to His word. (See Matthew 8:26-27.)
4. Jesus the Christ, the Son of God, has power over demons. They are subject to His word. (See Matthew 8:16; Luke 4:35,36,41.)

5. Christ is far above *all* principality, power, might, dominion, and every name that is named, not only in this world but also in that which is to come. All things are in subjection under His feet. All the hierarchies of the angelic world are under Him. (See Ephesians 1:20-23.)
6. The Son of God upholds *all* things by the words of His power. (Hebrews 1:3.)

Conclusion: *Jesus Christ, the Son of God, is omnipotent.*

B. Omniscience.
1. Jesus knows men's lives, even their secret history. (See John 4:16-19.)
2. Jesus knows the secret thoughts of men. He knew all men. He knew what was in man. (See Mark 2:8; Luke 5:22; and John 2:24-25.)
3. Jesus knew from the beginning that Judas would betray Him. Not only men's present thoughts but their future choices were known to Him. (See John 6:64.)
4. Jesus knew what men were doing at a distance. (See John 1:48.)
5. Jesus knew the future regarding not only God's acts, but also the minute

specific acts of men, even the fishes of the sea. (See Luke 5:4-6; Luke 22:10-12; and John 13:1.)

6. Jesus knew all things. In Him are hid all the treasures of wisdom and knowledge. (See John 16:30; 21:17; Colossians 2:3.)

Conclusion: *Jesus Christ is omniscient.*

C. Omnipresence.
   1. Jesus Christ is present in every place where two or three are gathered together in His name. (See Matthew 18:20.)
   2. Jesus Christ is present with everyone who goes forth into any part of the world to make disciples, etc. (See Matthew 28:20.)
   3. Jesus Christ is in each believer. (See John 14:20; 2 Corinthians 13:5.)
   4. Jesus Christ filleth all in all. (See Ephesians 1:23.)

Conclusion: *Jesus Christ is omnipresent.*

D. Eternal.
   1. Jesus is eternal. (See Isaiah 9:7; Micah 5:2; John 1:1; John 17:5; Colossians 1:17; and Hebrews 13:8.)

Conclusion: *The Son of God was from all eternity.*

E. Immutable.

   1. Jesus Christ is unchangeable. He not
      only always is, but always is *the same*.
      (See Hebrews 1:12; 13:8.)

Conclusion: Five or more distinctively divine attributes are ascribed to Jesus Christ, and *all the fullness of the Godhead is said to dwell in Him*. (See Colossians 2:9.)

III. Divine Offices

A. The Son of God, the eternal Word, the
   Lord, is Creator of all created things. (See
   John 1:3; Colossians 1:16; Hebrews 1:10.)

B. The Son of God is the preserver of all
   things. (See Hebrews 1:3.)

C. Jesus Christ had power on earth to forgive
   sins. (See Mark 2:5-10; Luke 7:48-50.)

D. Jesus Christ raised the dead. (See John
   6:39-44; 5:28-29.) Question: Did not Elijah
   and Elisha raise the dead? No, God raised
   the dead in answer to their prayer, but Jesus Christ will raise the dead by His own
   word. During the days of His humiliation,
   it was by prayer that Christ raised the
   dead.

E. Jesus Christ shall fashion anew the body of our humiliation into the likeness of His own glorious body. (See Philippians 3:21.)

F. Christ Jesus shall judge the living and the dead. (See 2 Timothy 4:1.)

G. Jesus Christ is the bestower of eternal life. (See John 10:28; 17:2.)

Conclusion: *Seven distinctively divine offices belong to Jesus Christ.*

IV. **Old Testament statements made distinctly about Jehovah God refer to Jesus Christ in the New Testament:**

A. Numbers 21:6-7. Compare 1 Corinthians 10:9.

B. Psalm 23:1; Isaiah 40:10-11. Compare John 10:11.

C. Psalm 102:24-27. Compare Hebrews 1:10-12.

D. Isaiah 3:10; 6:1. Compare John 12:37-41.

E. Isaiah 8:12-13. Compare 1 Peter 3:14-15.

F. Isaiah 8:13-14. Compare 1 Peter 2:7-8.

G. Isaiah 40:3-4. Compare Matthew 3:3; Luke 1:68-69, 76.

H. Isaiah 60:19; Zechariah 2:5. Compare Luke 2:32.

I. Jeremiah 11:20; 17:10. Compare Revelation 2:23.

J. Ezekiel 34:11-12,16. Compare Luke 19:10.

K. "Lord" in the Old Testament always refers to God except when the context clearly indicates otherwise. "Lord" in the New Testament always refers to Jesus Christ except where the context clearly indicates otherwise.

Conclusion: *Many statements in the Old Testament made distinctly of Jehovah God are taken in the New Testament to refer to Jesus Christ. In New Testament thought and doctrine Jesus Christ occupies the place that Jehovah occupies in Old Testament thought and doctrine.*

V. **Names of God the Father and Jesus Christ the Son coupled together**

A. 2 Corinthians 13:14.

B. Matthew 28:19.

C. 1 Thessalonians 3:11.

D. 1 Corinthians 12:4-6.

E. Titus 3:4-5. Compare Titus 2:13.

F. Romans 1:7. (See all the Pauline Epistles.)

G. James 1:1.

H. John 14:23, "we," i.e., **God and Jesus Christ.**

I. 2 Peter 1:1.

J. Colossians 2:2.

K. John 17:3.

L. John 14:1. Compare Jeremiah 17:5-7.

M. Revelation 7:10.

N. Revelation 5:13. Compare John 5:23.

Conclusion: *The name of Jesus Christ is coupled with that of God the Father in numerous passages in a way in which it would be impossible to couple the name of any finite being with that of the Deity.*

VI. Divine Worship is to be given to Jesus Christ.

A. Jesus Christ accepted without hesitation a worship which good men and angels declined with fear (horror). (See Matthew 4:9-10; Matthew 14:33; Matthew 28:8-9; Luke 24:52. Compare Acts 10:25-26; and Revelation 22:8-9.)

B. Prayer is to be made to Christ. (See Acts 7:59; 1 Corinthians 1:2; 2 Corinthians 12:8-9.)

C. It is God the Father's will that all men pay the same divine honor to the Son as to Himself. (See Psalm 45:11; John 5:23. Compare Revelation 5:8-9,12-13.)

D. The Son of God, Jesus, is to be worshipped as God by angels and men. (See Philippians 2:10-11; Hebrews 1:6. Compare Isaiah 45:21,23.)

Conclusion: *Jesus Christ is a Person to be worshipped by angels and men even as God the Father is worshipped*.

General Conclusion: By the use of numerous divine names, by attributing all the distinctively divine attributes, by the affirmation of several divine offices, by referring statements which in the Old Testament distinctly name Jehovah God as their subject to Jesus Christ in the New Testament, by coupling the name of Jesus Christ with that of God the Father in a way in which it would be impossible to couple that of any finite being with that of the Deity, and by the clear teaching that Jesus Christ should be worshipped even as God the Father is worshipped—in all these unmistakable ways, God's Word distinctly proclaims that Jesus Christ is a Divine Being and is indeed God.

One suggestion remains in regard to topical study. Get further subjects for topical study from your own book studies.

Chapter 4

BIOGRAPHICAL STUDY

A third method of study is the *biographical study*. This needs no definition. It consists in studying the life, work, and character of various persons mentioned in Scripture. It is really a special form of topical study and can be especially useful to the minister as he prepares his sermons. The following suggestions will help those who are not already experienced in this line of work.

1. Using *Strong's Concordance* collect all the passages in the Bible which mention the person to be studied.
2. Analyze the character of the person. This will require a repeated reading of the passages in which he is mentioned. This should be done with pencil in hand so that any characteristic may be noted at once.
3. Note the elements of power and success.
4. Note the elements of weakness and failure.
5. Note the difficulties overcome.

6. Note the helps to success.
7. Note the privileges abused.
8. Note the opportunities neglected.
9. Note the opportunities improved.
10. Note the mistakes made.
11. Note the perils avoided.
12. Make a sketch of the life in hand. Make it as vivid, living, and realistic as possible. Try to reproduce the subject as a real, living person. Note the place and surroundings of the different events, e.g., Paul in Athens, Corinth, or Philippi. Note the time relationships of different events. Very few people take notice of the rapid passage of time when they read the Acts of the Apostles. They regard events that are separated by years as following one another in close sequence. In this connection note the age or approximate age of the subject at the time of the events recorded.
13. Summarize the lessons we should learn from the story of this person's life.
14. Note the person's relationship to Jesus as a type of Christ (Joseph, David, Solomon, and others), a forerunner of Christ, a believer in Christ, an enemy of Christ, a servant of Christ, a brother of Christ (James and Jude), or a friend, etc.

Begin with some person who does not occupy too much space in the Bible, such as Enoch or Stephen. Of course many of the points mentioned above cannot be taken up with some characters.

Chapter 5

STUDY OF TYPES

ANALOGIES
FIGURATIVES

A fourth method of study is the *study of types*. It is both an interesting and instructive method of study. It shows us precious truths buried away in seemingly dry and meaningless portions of the Bible. This method of study is, however, greatly abused and overdone in some quarters. But that is no reason why we should neglect it altogether, especially when we remember that not only Paul, but Jesus, was fond of this method of study. The following methods may serve as principles to govern us in this study.

Be sure you have a Biblical authority for your supposed type. If one gives free rein to his suppositions, he can imagine types everywhere, even in places that neither the human nor the Divine Author of the book had any intention. Never say this is a type unless you can point to some clear passage of Scripture where types are definitely taught.

Begin with simple and evident types such as the

Passover (compare Exodus 12 with 1 Corinthians 5:7), the high priest, or the tabernacle.

Be on guard against the overstrained imagination. Anyone blessed with imagination and quickness of typical discernment will find his imagination running away unless he holds it in check.

In studying any passage where types may be suggested, look up all Scriptural references in a reliable concordance.

Study carefully the meaning of the names of persons and places mentioned. Bible names often have a deep and far-reaching suggestiveness. For example, Hebron, which means "joining together," "union," or "fellowship," is deeply significant when taken in connection with its history, as are all the names of the cities of refuge. Was it accidental that Bethlehem, the name of the place where the Bread of Life was born, means "house of bread"?

Chapter 6

STUDY OF BIBLICAL AND
CHRONOLOGICAL ORDER

A fifth method of Bible study is the old-fashioned method of *biblical order,* beginning at Genesis and going right on through to Revelation. This method has some advantages which no other method of study possesses.

Start at the beginning of this library of sixty-six books and read right through. It is important to master the Bible as a whole in order to understand the separate books in it.

There are advantages to studying the Bible in scriptural order. First, it is the only method by which you will get an idea of the Book as a whole. The more you know of the Bible as a whole, the better prepared you will be to understand any individual portion of it. Second, it is the only method by which you are likely to cover the whole Book and so take in the entire scope of God's revelation. This is a time-consuming, but rewarding way, to study the Bible.

Every part of God's Word is precious. Hidden

away in the most unexpected places such as 1 Chronicles 4:10, you will find priceless gems. It is also the best method to enable one to get hold of the unity of the Bible and its organic character.

The Bible is a many-sided book. It clearly teaches the Deity of Christ and insists on His real humanity. It exalts faith and demands works. It urges to victory through conflict and asserts most vigorously that victory is won by faith.

If you become too one-sided with any line of truth, the daily, orderly study of the Bible will soon bring you to some contrasted line of truth and back to proper balance. Some people have become mentally distracted through too much occupation with a single line of truth. Thoughtful study of the whole Bible is a great corrective to this tendency.

It would be good to have three methods of study in progress at the same time: First, the study of some book; second, the study of topics (perhaps topics suggested by the book studies); third, the study of the Bible in course. Every other method of study should be supplemented by studying the Bible in order.

Some years ago I determined to read a different version of the Bible and the New Testament in Greek through every year. It proved exceedingly profitable in my own studies.

Studying By Chronological Order

Another method of study is closely related to the

above method and has advantages of its own. It is studying the various portions of the Bible in their *chronological order*. In this way the Psalms are read in their historical settings, as are prophecies, epistles, etc.

Chapter 7

STUDY FOR PRACTICAL USE
IN DEALING WITH PEOPLE

The last method of study is the *study of the Bible for use in dealing with people.*

To study the Bible in this way, make as complete a classification as possible of all the different personalities that you find. Write the names of these various types at the head of separate sheets of paper or cards. Then begin reading the Bible through slowly. When you come to a passage that seems likely to prove useful in dealing with a certain personality type, write it down on a separate sheet. Go through the entire Bible in this way. Use special Bible markers in different colored inks or use different letters or symbols to represent the personalities. The best book is the one you organize yourself. The author's book, *How To Bring Men To Christ*, may give you some suggestions on how to begin.

The following list of types of people are suggestions to which you can add.

1. The careless and indifferent.
2. Those who wish to be saved but do not know how.
3. Those who know how to be saved but have difficulties. They may be further categorized with statements such as:

"I am too great a sinner."
"My heart is too hard."
"I must become better before I become a Christian."
"I am afraid I can't hold out."
"I am too weak."
"I have tried before and failed."
"I cannot give up my evil ways."
"I will be persecuted if I become a Christian."
"It will hurt my business."
"There is too much to give up."
"The Christian life is too hard."
"I am afraid of ridicule."
"I will lose my friends."
"I have no feeling."
"I have been seeking Christ but cannot find Him."
"God won't receive me."
"I have committed the unpardonable sin."
"It is too late."
"Christians are so inconsistent."
"God seems to me unjust and cruel."
"There are so many things in the Bible which I can't understand."
"There is someone I can't forgive."

Perhaps you will meet people who are cherishing false hopes. Their hope lies in being saved by a righteous life or by being saved by "trying to be a good Christian." They may "feel saved" because of a profesion of religion or church membership.

Others in your listings may include those who wish to put off the decision to be saved, such as Jews, Spiritualists, or Christian Scientists. You may also add to your list: the sorrowing, the persecuted, the discouraged, the despondent, or the worldly Christian.

The results of this work will be of incalculable value. You will get a new view of how perfectly the Bible is adapted to every man's need. Familiar passages of the Bible will take on new meaning as you see their relationship to the needs of men.

In seeking food for others, you will get a vast amount of material to use in sermons, in teaching, and in personal work. You will acquire a rare working knowledge of the Bible.

Chapter 8

FINAL SUGGESTIONS

Some suggestions remain to be given before we close this book.

Study The Bible Daily

Regularity counts more in Bible study than most people can imagine. The spasmodic student who sometimes gives a great deal of time to the study of the Word and at other times neglects it for days does not achieve the same results as the one who plods on regularly day by day. The Bereans were wise as well as "noble" in that they "searched the scriptures daily" (Acts 17:11).

A well-known speaker among Christian college students once remarked that he had been at many conventions and had received great blessings from them, but the greatest blessing he had ever received was from a convention where only four persons gathered together. These four had covenanted together to spend a certain portion of every day in

Bible study. Since that day much of his time had been spent in cars, in hotels, and at conventions; but he had kept that covenant. The greatest blessing that had come to him in his Christian life had come through this *daily* study of the Word.

Anyone who has tried it realizes how much can be accomplished by setting apart a fixed portion of each day for Bible study. You may study as little as fifteen or thirty minutes, but it is better to have an hour kept sacredly for that purpose under all circumstances.

Many will say, "I cannot spare the time." It will not do to study the Bible only when you feel like it or when you have leisure. You must have fixed habits if you are to study the Bible profitably. Nothing is more important than daily Bible study, and less important things must not take its place. What regularity in eating is to physical life, regularity in Bible study is to spiritual life. Fix upon some time, even if it is no more than fifteen minutes to start with and hold to it until you are ready to set a longer period.

Select The Correct Time

Don't put your Bible study off until nearly bedtime when your mind is drowsy. It is good to meditate on God's Word as you retire, but this is not the time for study. Bible study demands a clear mind. Don't take the time immediately after a heavy meal when you are mentally and physically sluggish. It is almost the unanimous opinion of those who have given this subject careful attention that the early hours of the day are the best for Bible study, if they can be free from interruption. Wherever possible, lock yourself in and lock the world out to concentrate fully on the Word of God.

Look For Jesus

We read of Jesus that "beginning at Moses and all the prophets, he expounded unto them in all the scriptures the things concerning himself" (Luke 24:27). Jesus Christ is the subject of the whole Bible, and He pervades the entire Book. Some of the seemingly driest portions become infused with a new life when we learn to see Christ in them. I remember in my early reading what a dull book Leviticus seemed; but it all became different when I learned to see Jesus in the various offerings and sacrifices, in the high priest and his garments, in the tabernacle and its furniture, and indeed everywhere. Look for Christ in every verse you study, and even the genealogies and the names of towns will begin to have beauty and power.

Memorize Scripture

The psalmist said, "Thy word have I hid in mine heart, that I might not sin against thee" (Psalms 119:11). There is nothing better to keep one from sinning than this. By the Word of God hidden in His heart, Jesus overcame the tempter. (See Matthew 4:4,7,10.)

But the Word of God hidden in the heart is good for other purposes than victory over sin. It is good to meet and expose error. It is good to enable one "to speak a word in season to him that is weary" (Isaiah 50:4). It is good for manifold uses, even "that the man of God may be perfect, thoroughly furnished unto all good works" (2 Timothy 3:17).

Memorize Scripture by chapter and verse. It is just as easy as memorizing a few words, and it is immeasurably more useful for practical purposes. Memorize Scripture in systematic form. Do not have a chaotic heap of texts in your mind, but pigeon-hole under appropriate titles the Scripture you store in memory. Then you can bring it out when you need it, without racking your brain. Many can stand up without a moment's warning and speak coherently and convincingly on any vital theme because they have a vast fund of wisdom in Scripture texts stored away in their mind in systematic form.

Utilize Spare Moments

Most of us waste too much time. Time spent traveling, waiting for appointments, or waiting for meals can be utilized in Bible study if you will carry a pocket Bible or pocket Testament. Or you can utilize the time to meditate upon texts already stored away in memory.

Henry Ward Beecher read one of the larger histories of England through while waiting day after day for his meals to be brought to the table. How many books of the Bible could be studied in the same way? A friend once told me about a man who had, in some respect, the most extraordinary knowledge of the Bible of any man he knew. This man was a junk dealer in a Canadian city. He kept a Bible open on his shelves; and during intervals of business, he pondered over the Book of God. The book became black from handling in such surroundings, but I have little doubt his soul became correspondingly white. No economy pays as does the economy of time, but there is no way of economizing time so thriftily as putting wasted moments into the study of or meditation upon the Word of God.